Simple

Family Traditions

(...and sautéed onions, too)

Linda J. Mitchell

♡ Enjoy creating your own special traditions!

Linda J Mitchell

ISBN: 151438101X
ISBN-13: 978-1514381014

CreateSpace Independent Publishing Platform
www.amazon.com

Edited by Laura Novia
Illustrated by Heath Hilliker

DEDICATION

To my three biggest inspirations:
Kevin, Cara and Greg
(Thanks, Bill)

Contents

Foreword

Having months earlier put my teaching career and supplies in storage, I boarded the plane with our new three-month-old son and headed off to meet my husband. Bill was already launched in his new job and in our new state. Hundreds of miles from friends, family and my previous identity, I arrived in a small, sleepy town on the shores of the Long Island Sound. It was September and New England was already starting to settle in for the long, gray winter ahead.

In an attempt to connect to the humanity around me, I joined Guilford, Connecticut's Newcomers Club. It would come to be one of the most important first steps I took on my journey through motherhood. Eight women sitting on the carpeted floors of each other's new homes, with infants in car seats beside us, was powerful stuff. We were all first-time mommies who had all left jobs and homes and given birth within the past twelve months. The collective hunger for friendship and parenting know-how bonded us quickly and deeply. In these new roles and locations, we shared our newest discoveries, fears and solutions; all while validating each other. We talked our heads off and it was a lifesaver for me.

This book is my attempt to share the kind of ideas, mostly pragmatic and simple, which one might learn amidst a playgroup or mom's lunch group. With much appreciation, I would like to thank the more than 40 women (some from that original playgroup) who made this book possible by allowing me to incorporate their family traditions into these chapters. This is not intended to be a book you follow to the letter. Rather, I hope it inspires you to consider simple acts that can strengthen your family bonds, whether initiated by a parent, aunt, cousin or grandparent. The ideas on these pages offer easy yet meaningful ways to underscore special moments and treasured relationships within your family dynamic.

Traditions need not be static or burdensome. With few exceptions, traditions should be held onto lightly so they may evolve naturally in concert with the ever-changing circumstances and characteristics of the family unit. To further underscore that point, I have purposely minimized the number of chapter headings so that this book reads more as an ongoing flow of possibilities. While the ideas contained within may reference an age or stage, most can easily be tweaked to work at many other ages and in a variety of situations. Just pick some of the ideas that especially appeal to you and make them your own.

As for the "sautéed onions" in the book title, when my children were young they preferred their foods to be simple, plain and not touching each other. As they have grown and their palates matured, I have been inspired to get creative and invent numerous quick, one-dish meals. Recently, my college daughter commented that nearly all the one-dish dinners I create start with sautéing a chopped onion. She quickly pronounced that this was our newest tradition! Just for fun, at the back of the book you will find several of these original recipes.

Never underestimate the impact of the simplest traditions. They create strong, continuous threads that will add to the fabric of your family's collective life experience and history. You cannot predict how an original and wonderful tradition may emerge. Sometimes a tradition is rooted in a pleasing pattern that you want to make a point to repeat; sometimes it grows out of addressing a particular need. Or perhaps it just comes from finding a great new idea or two in a simple book of shared experiences.

Birthdays

While wearing a little gold paper crown, complete with elastic under his chin, and intently sucking his pacifier, the first grandchild on my side of the family must have wondered when the excessive merriment over his first birthday would end and he could take a much needed nap. As we took yet one more photo of the birthday boy, his eyes flickered and his head dropped forward into the frosted cupcake on his highchair tray. Kevin couldn't fight the need to nap another second.

And so began the first foray into my perceived responsibility to validate my child's self-worth through the celebration of his birth day. Rare is the mom who hasn't entertained delusions of grandeur in planning a fabulous party for their precious offspring. You would be equally hard pressed to find a mom who hasn't heard the birthday party legends involving backyard pony rides with petting zoos or the birthday limo whisking the seven-year-old party girls to an upscale hotel for spa treatments. It can all be quite overwhelming and at times rather ridiculous.

Looking back, what are your clearest birthday memories? Do you remember how it felt answering the door to find an invited guest with a brightly wrapped gift in hand, the fun of being the center of attention, those smiling faces singing "Happy Birthday" somewhat off key? Perhaps your most vivid memories include receiving the toy your parents wouldn't buy for you, getting an upset stomach from too many M&M's, water balloon fights, the family dog dressed in the gift bows or having to write those darn thank you notes.

Sometimes what goes wrong at a birthday party can be more fun and memorable than what was planned. At other times what goes wrong makes for a big disappointment and a parental headache in the moment, but years later can provide a riotous family tale. I have hosted birthday parties where the piñata wouldn't break, the craft project didn't stay glued together, the surprise party was no surprise, the homemade obstacle course became way out of control, the cake didn't get served before the guests were starting to head home and the dog got sick from all the crumbs. And yet surprisingly, I have always been considered one of the "organized" moms when it came to parties.

Of course in the end it all worked out as each person still turned another year older. The lesson to be learned about throwing birthday parties is that regardless of the ages involved, keep it simple and add some humor. Don't create birthday traditions that are so detailed and rigid that their successful implementation becomes complicated and burdensome. Have some fun considering the ideas that follow and then come up with hybrids that fit your personal style. When it comes to birthday celebrations, don't stop being whimsical just because the guest of honor is celebrating double digits. When you find a birthday tradition that seems geared towards a child, consider adjusting the idea or theme for a birthday boy or girl of any age!

Birthday Traditions

Write a special note to the birthday person to acknowledge their accomplishments and special experiences of the past year, while offering some wishes for the year ahead.

****

Find or make a wildly colorful, printed tablecloth as a zany way to underscore a birthday celebration at meal time. Such a tablecloth also makes a great gift idea to help another family launch its own new tablecloth tradition.

****

For a "sweet 16" birthday, have a treasure hunt of 16 written clues for 16 little surprises hidden throughout the house.

****

Personalize a birthday cake with small plastic items from a dollar store to reflect the birthday person's hobbies, favorite color, sports team, etc. Also, find a way to add their name.

The night before the birthday, secretly decorate the kitchen table with streamers and balloons so it's the first thing the birthday person sees in the morning. Set the table with a little gift to start the day. Decorations can be more or less creative or silly, and vary greatly from year to year.

****

Favorite birthdays often have an element of surprise. This could be an unexpected party location, unexpected guests, a surprise theme or just hidden birthday greetings or little gifts in places that will be discovered throughout the day.

****

Before a busy day takes everyone in different directions, first thing in the morning have the whole family jump onto the birthday person's bed with cards and gifts to acknowledge their special day.

****

Gather a few baby photos or other childhood memorabilia of the birthday person and use as the kitchen table centerpiece, or as a decoration on a mantel or shelf.

****

Each year, have the family look together through an early photo album to help the guest of honor feel particularly cherished.

Buy a huge, colorful "Happy Birthday" poster from a card shop or teachers' store, or better yet make your own. Hang it up on the refrigerator or kitchen door for the entire week preceding a birthday.

****

The night before the birthday, tie a long string to the child's bedroom doorknob. Once awake, they follow the string through the house to find their birthday gifts. The best gift is the last one, waiting in their seat at the kitchen table.

****

As a group, call long distance family members and spontaneously sing "Happy Birthday" to them the instant they answer the phone. No matter how old the birthday person, you will hear their smile over the phone. Be sure to pass the phone around so each person also has the chance to offer a personal birthday greeting.

****

Have a family dinner to celebrate on the actual birth date.

****

Make the person's favorite dinner and eat in the dining room, using nice dishes, cloth napkins and simple decorations to make it feel fancy. After the birthday meal, take everyone out to a movie or special event.

Make a monetary donation to a charity that was relevant
to a deceased family member on the anniversary
of their birthday.

****

For a milestone birthday, have each member of the family
make a list of "Ten Things I Love About You." Type them
onto brightly colored paper and cut them apart. The night
before the big day, tuck these small slips of paper all around
the house (by their toothbrush, taped to the bottle of orange
juice, laptop, steering wheel, etc.). During dinner the
birthday person guesses the author of each comment found.

Afterwards, gather all the comments into a small album with
a photo of the birthday person and each of the contributors,
entitle it: "Things We Love About You."

****

To help keep the memory alive of an extra-special relative,
start a tradition of having ice cream for lunch on what would
have been their birthday. During the ice cream feast,
be sure to share stories and anecdotes about the
loved one's life and interests.

****

Give each person in the family a shoe box (decorating the
outside is optional) to store their favorite birthday cards and
family notes. Be sure to date the back of each card and
be selective about what to save.

Have the same family-favorite breakfast on all birthday mornings. A delicious coffee cake and hard boiled eggs, prepared the night before, is a popular and easy breakfast.

****

Use a special plate for the birthday king or queen; it can be wacky and colorful or have a message on it like "You're Special." Such plates are great gifts for other households.

****

Regardless of the birthday person's age, wrap some gifts in the Sunday comics or use youthful wrapping paper with themes such as Disney or Sesame Street characters. Homemade handprint wrapping paper is another big hit. Be sure to have the artists autograph it.

****

Always make homemade frosting for the cake.

****

Use old family photographs to create homemade birthday cards. Cut out the head of the sender from an old photograph and use it to create a new scene. If the face is glued into the cockpit of an airplane drawing, the caption could read, "I'm flying by to wish you a happy birthday." Parachutes, boats, bees, birds, cars, trucks and animals are only some of the categories that lend themselves to a catchy birthday message accompanying a funny scene using a photo face.

Don't underestimate the memories made when everyone wears a party hat at cake time. Buy simple ones at a party store or let each person decorate a large rectangle of paper, later rolled and stapled into a classic cone shape. Decorated paper plates tied on with crepe paper streamers can make funny party hats, too. Another idea is to have a party hat box that contains all kinds of dress-up hats for the guests, but only one crown for the birthday person.

****

If you have enough time and courage, invite the honoree to pick all the meals for the special day. Or, have them only choose the dinner menu and cake/frosting flavors.

****

Have the number of party balloons equal the birthday age, plus one to grow on.

****

Take siblings of the birthday child to a drugstore or greeting card store to purchase a small item for the sibling's birthday. As children get older, they can use their own allowance to purchase a simple, thoughtful gift for their brother or sister.

****

For young children, buy a new hardback book to read-aloud at their party. Later, add it to the birthday child's own book collection, as a keepsake of their special day. Be sure to inscribe the inside book cover with your birthday greeting, the date and your signature.

****

Turn the birthday person's bedroom door into a huge personalized greeting card. Get everyone involved in creating a unique birthday collage by adding notes, drawings, photos, magazine clippings and streamers to the door. Photograph the finished product and use it as the opening page of a mini birthday album.

****

There is no reason to only have birthday candles on the cake. Start the special day with birthday candles lit on whatever is for breakfast, and don't forget to sing "Happy Birthday."

****

For durability, use scraps of fabric or felt and create a large family birthday banner to string up each week of a birthday.

****

Each year, create three coupons for the birthday person that grants them three wishes for simple activities they would most enjoy over the upcoming year.

In advance of the big day, a birthday journal can be passed around to family and friends, for each person to write a brief message. Eventually the child will have a journal that is brimming over with a collection of fun and loving comments from those dearest to them.

****

Head out for a birthday breakfast together prior to school or work.

****

Start with vanilla frosting and then add food dye to create the birthday person's favorite color for the icing.

****

As an adult, celebrate your birth date by going to donate blood and help save someone else's life.

****

When a child is born, start a birthday time capsule. This can be done by a parent, grandparent or other special person. Begin with a baby photo and small piece of memorabilia from the day the child was born. Each year add to the box one photo and one small item representing a current aspect of the child's life, until the child is old enough to choose their own item for inclusion. The box remains with the person who started the collection until the child's 21st birthday when the time capsule is gifted to them.

Your *Birthday* Traditions

Reaching Out

There I sat Indian-style on the floor of our Levittown ranch-style house, carefully clipping cartoons from my mom's stack of *Good Housekeeping* magazines. This is my earliest, firsthand memory of my mother's kindness to others outside our immediate family. She would collect one-frame cartoons and then glue them into expired, blank calendar books. When a page was turned there would be a lovely photograph preprinted by the manufacturer on the left-hand page and a cartoon or two glued over the days of the week on the right-hand page. She made these "books" filled with lighthearted cartoons to have on-hand when a friend was recovering from a prolonged illness or surgery, hoping to add a little humor to their road to recovery. We probably only completed about a handful of these, but I remember thinking how easy and fun it was to do something nice for someone else.

Establishing family traditions that nurture a perspective on how we should treat one another is a powerful means to developing generous and kind individuals. This is an area in which adult role models reign supreme. Be sure your family is aware of your good deeds and whenever possible get them involved too. When making "Thinking of You" cookies for a friend in need, see who else in the family could help bake or package the cookies, and be sure to have everyone sign the greeting card. When a family member is under the weather, encourage other members to assume some of his or her chores, bring them a hot drink, share a stuffed animal for comfort or make a get well picture. Regularly put a friendly note of encouragement on a bathroom mirror, in a lunch bag, a suitcase or briefcase. Create a "Welcome Home" sign for a special return. And if you really want to teach a tradition of kindness, figure out how to get all the family members involved with the care of the family pet, and then share your genius with the rest of us!

There have never been more places or ways to be involved in established charitable causes and organizations. These offer great possibilities for family togetherness and teachable moments. However, I believe the kindness and respect we demonstrate within our immediate family builds the strongest base from which to develop our own personal traditions of generosity. Charity should begin at home, with those who are nearest and dearest to us. Unfortunately, in reality we sometimes indulge our emotions more at home than anywhere else as it is the safest place for such behavior. After all, parents will continue to feed, clothe and shelter their offspring regardless of bad attitudes or mood swings. Siblings will certainly have highs and lows; but at the end of the day they are still blood relatives and connected forever by shared histories. So let's get on with the lifelong pursuit of being our finest selves and consciously look for ways to act with kindness both inside our family and outside in the larger community. There can never be enough kindness in the world, so here are some proven ways to inspire you and your family to reach out.

Reaching Out Traditions

Teach your children to have a goal of making someone's day, each day. It can be as simple as just smiling and saying "Hi" or "Have a nice day" to a passerby. Those simple words could be the nicest words that person receives all day.

****

Have a special family get well token that rotates to the bedside table of whoever is sick in bed. A small ceramic or stuffed animal, or a little angel figurine, will do the job.

****

If both parents are going out of town and the child is staying with a sitter or grandparent, pack a "Surprise-a-Day" grab bag. Each day the child picks one surprise, without peeking. Once the bag is empty, the parents are due home. It helps young children to be reminded of their parents' love while also giving them a sense of time.

****

Whenever a child needs uplifting, find a special quote, poem or Bible verse and secretly tape it to their bathroom mirror,

or leave it on their pillow. A laminated copy is an excellent
item to add to the suitcase of a child heading off
to a sleep-away camp.

****

Regularly move around your framed family photos, taking
turns placing the picture of one family member in a place
that especially stands out. It will be particularly meaningful
to do when a child comes for a visit, is going through a
difficult time or is celebrating a special occasion.

****

Have your family routinely go through their outgrown
clothes and toys to donate to those less fortunate
in the community. Together, bag and deliver them.

****

If a child is home sick from school for several days,
consider buying several kid-friendly magazines or comic
books. Having Tootsie Pops always on-hand can be
a tradition for soothing a sore throat and
temporarily lifting spirits.

****

Bake a favorite cookie recipe (like oatmeal chocolate chip)
with help from the family. Together, determine who most
needs some cheer and send the cookies via mail or leave on
a friend's doorstep with a little note.

When a dear friend is seriously ill or recovering from a loss, invite your mutual friends over to your home to read aloud and record favorite poems or prayers. A printed copy of what everyone shared can be included with the recording being delivered to the friend in need.

****

Send personalized M&M's or chocolate bars, greeting cards with recordable messages, or best of all use thumbprint "bugs" to illustrate a special message to a loved one in need of cheering up or congratulations.

****

When a beloved pet dies, put the remains in a box and bury it deep in a place where the soil won't be disturbed, such as under a special tree. Have everyone contribute a few words to a spontaneous prayer of thanksgiving for the joy the pet has added to the family's life. End the ceremony with an enthusiastic group "Amen!" and a big family hug.

****

Once a year, have your children help plan and execute a collection drive for a local charity. Together they can make fliers to take to neighbors, using your garage or porch as the drop-off site. The excitement will grow as the requested items (i.e., canned goods, diapers, gently worn winter coats) start coming in. Load everyone into the car when it is time to deliver the donations to the chosen organization.

Regardless of age, have everyone sign the greeting cards that are sent from your family. The youngest can scribble their name or have their hand traced. Encourage older children to write a sentence or two. For a card to an immediate family member have plenty of card-making art supplies available, or encourage children to use their allowance to purchase a card and add a personal message.

****

Make every effort to role model generosity by sharing your flowers, vegetables, old magazines, used books or home-baked goods with family and friends. Random acts of kindness are contagious! Is there a senior citizen or single parent living in your neighborhood who would appreciate a serving or two of your homemade soup?

****

Provide an older child with a gift of two tickets to an event of their liking, so they can invite a friend to join them. It feels good to invest in their friendships while also providing a special opportunity for someone else.

****

Make a habit of saying "Please" and "Thank you" easily and often. Parents leading by example is particularly powerful in establishing this tradition.

Before leaving home for a business trip, write a short note for each day you will be gone, labeled with the day of the week it should be read.

****

Once or twice a year, bring the whole family together to bake cookies or make small greeting cards to be added to the trays of your local Meals on Wheels program. Be sure to check first to determine what is allowable.

****

Pay it forward at a drive-thru fast food restaurant by also paying for the person's order in the car behind you.

****

Anytime your family throws a party, invite guests to bring canned goods for your local food bank rather than bring hostess gifts.

****

Have a special stuffed animal that only comes out for a visit when mom or dad is out of town.

****

When possible, anonymously pick up the check for a uniformed American military person's small purchase.

Good News Mondays: tell the family a news story regarding someone's generous act of kindness. It serves to remind everyone of the potential for compassion in everyday life and helps combat all the bad news with which we are constantly bombarded.

****

Put a glass jar in the kitchen for everyone's loose change. Once it is full, the family decides which charity should be the recipient of the funds.

****

Every so often, proclaim one day of the weekend as the "Giving Day." Each member of the family determines an act of kindness they will do that day for a fellow family member. They may ask for ideas from that person, but in the end it is their decision on what they choose to do. It could be anything from cleaning a bike, raking the yard, taking the dog on a long walk, cleaning out a closet, etc. Each time, rotate who helps who.

****

Run a neighborhood drive each August to collect needed supplies for a local school. Many schools are in desperate need of basic supplies, backpacks and gym equipment.

****

Find ways to help neighbors who are out of town, by collecting mail and newspapers and watering plants.

Be sure children are aware of the outreach programs provided by your place of worship. Beginning in first grade, encourage them to help support these by adding a few of their own coins to the collection plate during the services they attend.

****

Develop the tradition of writing thank you notes for gifts received without the person present.

****

At the start of each new year, have a family discussion to choose a non-profit cause to become involved with as a family for the next twelve months. It can be something in the local community or something on a global level.

****

Participate as a family in two local 5K walks each year to support worthwhile charitable causes.

****

When grocery shopping, purchase non-perishable "buy one, get one free" items whenever possible. Add the free items to a collection bin at home - once full, deliver the items to your local food pantry.

Your *Reaching Out* Traditions

_____
_____
_____
_____
_____
_____
_____
_____
_____
_____
_____
_____
_____
_____
_____
_____
_____
_____
_____
_____
_____
_____
_____
_____
_____
_____
_____
_____

FAMILY Time

It seemed like such a good idea at the time. It was late March in Connecticut and I was very much in need of something other than the seemingly endless, dreary winter weather on which to focus my energy. In a flash of inspiration, I decided to surprise my family of three with a Hawaiian picnic, set out on a beach towel in front of a roaring fireplace. I went about specially preparing an appropriately themed meal, which included ham, lots of pineapple and a colorful plastic lei for each guest. But despite my best efforts, our five-year-old son was unimpressed and found nothing on the menu worth eating. As the meal collapsed I fought back tears. Clearly, I needed an early spring.

It's not that the luau wasn't a good idea. But as a retired teacher and new mom, my hopes had been too high: a culturally relevant meal with educational opportunities and my son's enthusiastic cooperation! Consequently, my thoughts of Asian, French or Mexican themed meals were indefinitely postponed. Perhaps on a different day, at a different child's age, with a different set of expectations and with a generous dose of humor, it could have been a hit. Rule One: Don't take it to heart if what seems like a brilliant new family tradition falls flat on its face. Keep your sense of humor and try again. Later that week, I had my fellow playgroup moms in stitches as I described the miserably failed luau, and that was worth something.

Rule Two: Capitalize on naturally occurring events that could warrant repeating. One day when my sister came to visit our then family of four, an unexpected but wonderful new tradition was spontaneously born. At the time, our oldest child was a seven-year-old boy highly infatuated with trucks and Legos. Cara, his little sister, was four years old and loved her stuffed animals and baby dolls. Sometimes she would have a dolly tea party complete with her pink plastic china service atop her child-sized Fisher Price table with its little matching chairs. On this particular day, my sister decided to join the tea party already in progress. She donned an exaggerated English accent, held her pinkie up as she sipped "tea" and balanced on a little chair while asking our daughter all kinds of silly questions. Needless to say, our son was soon at the table too. The three of them chatted, sipped apple juice, munched on cookies and laughed and laughed. From that day forward, when Aunt Laura arrived for a visit, a tea party was the top priority. This continued for several years, even when the children were no longer having tea parties on their own. It was a magical tradition that had a healthy run. Perhaps some of the suggestions that follow can spark a few new traditions in your home.

Family Time Traditions

Each summer, divide the family into two teams, having a mini-golf tournament that lasts until the end of summer. Find a goofy statue to serve as the annual rotating trophy.

Dinner on Sunday nights can serve as a family meeting where everyone discusses the upcoming week. It can also be a time for each person to share one thing from the previous week for which they are thankful.

****

Every so often, add something to a child's school lunch or backpack such as a single comic strip, a knock-knock joke or an interesting animal fact. Use the comic strips from the newspaper or find inexpensive books that you can cut up. Besides reminding them you are thinking of them, it gives them something fun to share with friends.

****

The first snow day off from school means cookies, hot cocoa and a group effort to build the best snowman ever.

****

Jigsaw puzzles are a wonderful way to have casual conversation across all ages. At large family gatherings have a new puzzle spread out on a central table, ready for anyone to lend a hand throughout the get-together. Flipping the pieces face-up can involve the youngest.

****

Make handprint slabs of each family member for your garden or walkway and don't forget the paw prints of the furry members of your family.

On that momentous day when your teenager's braces come off, present the ecstatic child with a small gift bag of previously off-limit sticky stuff such as Swedish Fish, sugar-free gum, and of course a colorful new toothbrush.

****

Each summer, it's off to a local farm for blueberry picking. Bring along small snacks and drinks to keep everyone energized. That evening, enjoy a homemade blueberry dessert. Repeat again for strawberry season!

****

Give each child their own recipe card box and from time to time add index cards of simple recipes and family favorites. As they get older, they can add recipes for dishes they are learning to cook themselves or for ones they have invented.

****

On the occasion of getting a driver's license, give the new driver a personally themed or initialed key chain and add a mini-light, a key to the house and possibly a key to a family car.

****

Start a tradition of a favorite family snack associated with special activities. Perhaps trail mix always accompanies bike rides, Starburst on the ski lift, Life Savers for boat rides and carrot sticks when hiking.

Friday night is Game Night with board games and card games galore. Rotate weekly who gets to pick the game. Or, have a jar full of game choices and have one randomly picked.

****

You can make dinner time more engaging and keep everyone at the table a little longer by playing "High-Low." Each person has to tell the high point and low point of their day, but tests, gym class, recess and lunch are prohibited answers. This is really fun and interesting with all ages.

****

Discover a universally favorite family restaurant and make it the go-to destination for special family celebrations.

****

Celebrate a "Backwards Day" that begins with a dinner menu for breakfast. The best part is having breakfast food at dinner time with everyone wearing pajamas and slippers.

****

Parents take turns reading aloud to their children at bedtime using a book series. As they get older, parents and children can alternate reading a page or chapter aloud. This also provides a wonderful opportunity to introduce short stories, mythology and poems into the mix.

Choose a simple treat to enjoy together following each
school concert, season opener or other noteworthy
school event. It could be going out for fruit smoothies
or heading home for chips and salsa.

****

Pick one funny television series to watch together
as a family each week and don't forget the popcorn.
Laughing together is a great family bonding activity.

****

Have family team tournaments of "Hang Man."

****

Make walking together a simple and healthy tradition.
Each Thanksgiving after the big meal, everyone heads out
the door (dogs included) for some fresh air. The routine of
a weekly Sunday afternoon walk is another tradition that
increases fitness and communication.

****

Once a week bring an egg timer to the dinner table.
Allowing no one to interrupt, each person gets a turn talking
on a topic of their choice until the timer buzzes.
Parents get a turn, too.

In the fall, find a huge corn maze at a local farm in your area.
Have an annual challenge of kids versus adults to see which
group can find their way out first.

****

When it comes to the Tooth Fairy, just a pinch
of glitter left behind goes a long way to dazzle imaginations.

****

Keep a jar handy for loose change and every once in a while
ask everyone at the table to guess its value. Whoever's guess
is closest gets to keep the coins, or choose a charitable cause
as the recipient, or do a little of both.

****

Consider displaying children's artwork everywhere; frame,
laminate, or just tape the art to a wall, shelf or window.
Clip it on an indoor clothesline. Use magnetic frames on the
refrigerator. Regularly change what's exhibited. What better
way to say, "You are special and I love what you create,"
than to have your child's artwork where they can see it
and know that their creativity is valued.

****

Find one main mealtime a week that is protected by all
as special family time. This also provides a meaningful
opportunity to encourage kids to help cook and
contribute to the meal's clean up.

Some children want to leave a note asking Tabitha the Tooth Fairy all kinds of questions. Be sure the response is written using very small letters on very small paper. Most importantly, keep all the notes and responses so that you will later have the collection to share as a childhood treasure.

****

Anytime the family is having a big fuss, just yell "Dairy Queen." Everyone feels better after an ice cream break, whether you eat out or bring it in.

****

Have a fun phrase to use at the end of phone calls between family members. It can be as simple as "Love you!" or as silly as "Later Alligator!" These should evolve with different family stages and ages.

****

Once a college has been chosen, surprise the freshman-to-be by covering a bedroom door, window or refrigerator with taped-on scenes and phrases obtained from the school's pamphlets and website. Add personal notes of congratulations as well as a baby picture and a high school graduation photo, to underscore how far they have come.

****

Before moving to a new house, have your family walk together through the old house saying "goodbye" and "thank you" to each room.

Each year on the birthday of a deceased parent, celebrate "Sibling Day" by having the adult children meet for a special day or meal together, or simply enjoy a lengthy, long-distance phone conversation to recall the life and times of their loved one.

****

Come up with a great family motto.
Invite the children to create a family crest, too.

****

Once a month, enjoy a family "Mystery Outing." Mom and Dad can take turns planning these little surprise activities.

****

At a pet's funeral, have each family member share a favorite memory.

****

Establish your family's signature gift (a music box, small clock, favorite children's book) to give every time a new member of the extended family is born. Consider adding a coupon for one session of babysitting.

****

Every spring have a family planting day to add flowering plants to a small garden or window box, begin kitchen herbs in small indoor pots or just plant seedlings in an ice cube tray for later transfer to a larger container or garden.

Once a month, each family member plans and cooks a meal, with other family members as the support crew.

****

Each summer attend a family-friendly music festival. Bring along a blanket, picnic and simple games.

****

If you are a long-distance grandparent, consider finding a small, collectable item you can bring to each grandchild on every visit to help them build a fun collection. You could bring a silver dollar, foreign postage stamps, marbles, seashells or even postcards from various locations; just choose a category that would be fun for both of you.

****

When driving home from a nearby location, play Left-Right-Center. Have the children dictate the first few driving directions for the driver, and then challenge the driver to find the way back home from the last instruction.

****

At the start of each season, create a one-page newsletter giving updates on the family's activities and include drawings or notes by the children. Long-distance family members will be delighted to receive these treasures.

Your *Family Time* Traditions

_____

_____

_____

_____

_____

_____

_____

_____

_____

_____

_____

_____

_____

_____

_____

_____

_____

_____

_____

_____

_____

_____

_____

_____

_____

_____

_____

_____

SCHOOL *Days*

On the first day of a new school year, you can pretty well guess the birth order of the various children anxiously waiting at the bus stop. Firstborns are usually accompanied by Mom for weeks, while second-born children are often turned over to the older sibling's hand around Day Four. As for the third, fourth and beyond in the birth order, they have already learned bus stop basics having been regularly pulled from their warm beds, still in jammies, to join Mom or Dad in escorting older siblings. New backpacks, fresh shoes and first day jitters all add to the anticipation of a new school year and the message that school is a big deal.

In elementary school, we lived in the second to the last house from the corner, also known as the formal demarcation line of who got a bus ride to and from school. No children lived in the corner house, so for years I was the furthest walker of my large neighborhood. Incredibly, I can't remember ever *not* walking to elementary school. It wasn't as if at a certain age or grade my parents said, "Okay, now you are old enough to come to and from school on your own." I was making the 20-plus minute trek each way beginning in first grade, with the only adult interaction being the two crossing guard women who were stationed at cross streets when school was finally in sight. If rain was in the forecast, I was handed an umbrella that morning with my lovingly made brown bag lunch. There was no pick-up at the school's front door due to inclement weather for me, unless the lightning was really close. This is despite the fact that my mom was a stay-at-home, conservative parent and I was her precious daughter and first-born. I remember feeling lonely at times, exhausted at others, sometimes empowered, and always there was daydreaming. Clearly I survived and am still good at a daydream now and then, but walking – lots and lots of walking, is one of my most vivid memories related to elementary school. My sister, younger by four years, also had the privilege of this family tradition that helped to build self-reliance.

When I did move on to middle school and buses, it was with mixed emotions. There were certainly pros and cons to both walking or being bused to school. But one thing is sure, the challenges presented by each helped me in different ways to grow up and learn about managing myself. As in many things in life, it is the secondary aspects of an official experience that can teach you important hidden lessons.

As for traditions beyond walking to school, I fondly remember my mother taking us on our annual August trek into Philadelphia to buy school clothes, where my dad enjoyed an employee discount at the massive John Wanamaker's department store in Center City. If it wasn't sold there, I wasn't going to be wearing it. Beyond being physically outfitted for the year ahead, I would say there was a continuous tradition of expectation in my family: "We just ask you to do your best." Traditions come in many forms, some literal, some not so much. Perhaps some of the following ideas will strike a chord and inspire you to try a handful with your family.

School Time Traditions

The week before a new school year starts, have the entire family sit together to watch old family movies or leaf through family photo albums. Seeing how far they have come helps children feel more confident about handling the new experience ahead, whether it be first grade or freshman year at college that awaits them.

****

Develop your own annual celebration of School Year's Eve!

****

On the night before school starts, have the tradition of reading aloud Dr. Seuss' book, *Oh, The Places You'll Go*.

****

The first day back to school is a nice chance for Mom and Dad to have their own tradition of going out together for breakfast in celebration of their children's newest milestone.

****

Each year, just prior to the start of school, have children do a big clean-up in their bedrooms (parent help is available). Keep in mind what may be good for donating.

****

Be sure to take a photo on every first day of school with the student holding their own homemade sign announcing the new grade level and year. Using a chalkboard can be a fun alternative. In advance of a child starting at a new school, take a photo of them standing with the official school sign and post it on their bedroom door to build enthusiasm.

****

Prior to the school year, take a younger student out to buy a stuffed animal to be the year's "study buddy." Together with your child, set-up and organize their study space for the year, which includes the new friend.

****

One week before the start of school, host a picnic for your child to reconnect with schoolmates, helping to reduce first day jitters. Have lots of outdoor games available.

****

Put a note in the lunchbox or send a text to their phone that you can't wait to hear all about their first day of school. Make extra time to sit down and share a healthy snack while getting an update on their big day.

****

For the first weeks of school, have a parent or older sibling work quietly near the student doing homework to encourage a pattern of concentration and focus. This is a great excuse for Mom or Dad to enjoy some reading time of their own.

As your child heads out to school, remind them each day to "Ask one question today."

****

Friday is Fact Night at the dinner table. Have each person take a turn sharing something they learned during the past week. This is an opportune time for adults to bring current events to the discussion and to also help foster respect for differing opinions.

****

Make a special dinner or dessert to help celebrate the start of a new school year. A small wrapped school-related gift can be fun, such as a new calendar, colored pencils, a cool new pen or themed notebook.

****

From kindergarten to grade 12, equate the first day of school with a batch of their favorite cookies waiting for them at home, along with your enthusiasm. If a child is away at school, mail the cookies with a note.

****

Establish the "End-of-School Sleepover." On the last day of school, allow your child to invite several friends to a sleepover and celebrate the end of the school year. No formal activities need to be planned, just encourage a lot of outside games and end the evening with a movie and popcorn at home.

School's out! Take kids of all ages to a bookstore or library to stock-up on summer reading. Stop at a park or other reading-friendly location to quietly dive into the new reads.

****

Create a one-page "Favorites" form for your child to complete at the end of each school year, keeping them all in a three ring notebook. The "Favorites" list might include: book title, TV show, sports team, best friends, musical group, movie, school subject, hobby, family activity, food, teacher, and what they want to be when they grow-up. This becomes a fantastic time capsule and they will love looking back at their answers over the years.

****

Chronologically place one school photograph (kindergarten to grade 12) along with an inspirational quote per single page of a small scrapbook. Use the last pages for your family's handwritten messages of congratulations along with several photographs of the high school graduation.

****

Always have pancakes and bacon for the first breakfast of summer vacation.

****

Find a book program at your library or local bookstore that rewards students for reading a certain number of books over summer vacation. If you don't find one, make up your own. Ten books over a summer is a solid goal that earns a treat.

Upon request by the child and within reasonable circumstances, one "play hooky" day (a.k.a. Mental Health Day) per school year is allowed.

****

Create a one-of-a-kind quilt or wall hanging by sewing together square pieces of fabric from the graduating senior's T-shirts to represent past activities, schools and hobbies.

****

Present the new high school graduate with a handmade booklet of redeemable coupons for a batch of cookies, a care package for exams, a holiday-themed box or a Wild Card box to be mailed to them at college, upon request.

****

Buy a high quality photo album or scrapbook and emboss it with the child's name. As they grow up create a two-page spread to represent each year of the child's life, culminating with high school graduation. A photo album is always a welcome gift.

****

Leave behind a small box of goodies when dropping off a big kid for another year at college. Simple snacks, gift cards, photos, homemade treats, a few extra dollars, etc., will all be much appreciated.

When a child goes off to college, surprise them with a few framed photos that could include immediate family members, a favorite vacation shot and a photo of the family pet sitting in the child's bedroom at home.

****

For a child in college, occasionally fill a box with fun things for your student and their roommates. The goodies can relate to a holiday like Halloween (plastic spiders, fake webs, mini orange lights, candy) or "just because" (granola bars, microwave popcorn, trail mix, roll of quarters for laundry, etc.).

****

Establish your own family book club. Look for a simple book that everyone can read and afterwards briefly discuss. With a wide range of ages, another option is to let individuals choose their own book to read and later review it aloud for the whole family.

****

To promote lifelong learning, make it a tradition to visit historical sites, museums, art galleries and nature facilities as family outings.

****

At the end of each school year, have your child write a short thank you note to the teacher of their choice.

Your *School Time* Traditions

_____

_____

_____

_____

_____

_____

_____

_____

_____

_____

_____

_____

_____

_____

_____

_____

_____

_____

_____

_____

_____

_____

_____

_____

_____

_____

Vacations

The single most important element to building vacation traditions is simply to have a vacation in the first place. Regardless of everyone's age and stage, stay firm in your conviction that whether a vacation takes you far or keeps you close to home, it is an unmatched opportunity to build a tradition of family togetherness.

While in middle school, my parents decided our family of four should take a road trip to Williamsburg, Virginia, during a long fall weekend. I still have a few mental snapshots from that history-filled trip. But what remains more keenly etched in my memory is how for weeks in advance I squirreled away quarters, enabling me to make a call each evening on the hotel pay phone and complain to my boyfriend about how terribly bored I was. In hindsight, I'm grateful my parents dragged me along and didn't allow my limited perspective to dictate my level of participation.

This was even truer when I was in high school and my family had the opportunity to visit Switzerland and I begged to be left at home. Can you imagine! My teenage self was hormonally driven to be resistant to family togetherness, and the idea of being so independent from my family unit was heady stuff. In the end, they insisted I go and were generally good-natured about ignoring my occasional pout. I have to admit that on some level I was secretly relieved they cared so much to insist on my inclusion. And it certainly was an amazing trip. Of course, I didn't admit any of that to my parents until several years later.

Whether it be a mini vacation or an overnight in a tent in the backyard, a road trip adventure or an extravagant trip abroad, the key is to be together. Next you will find helpful hints for travel traditions that emphasize fun.

Vacation Traditions

Post a simple handwritten invitation on each person's bedroom door to help build the anticipation while also serving as a reminder to save the vacation dates.

****

Start an on-going road trip journal of each state visited which chronicles unique natural and manmade landmarks, the state flag, the official state tree, bird and so forth.

****

On route to your regular destination, like the local beach or hiking trail, determine a special stop along the way that is always included in the experience and much anticipated. Perhaps a frozen yogurt or hot dog stop?

****

Be sure to never leave home without a deck of cards.

For an extended car ride, have everyone help find license plates from different states. Maintain one master list and see how many states are found before returning back home. Determine whose guess is closest to the final total and therefore earns the winner's title – until next time!

****

Bring along a large photo of the family pet that couldn't make the trip. Then include this likeness of the furry family member in some of the vacation photos.

****

Have a countdown calendar, marking off each day as it gets closer to departure. Everyone loves the anticipation of an upcoming adventure.

****

Regardless of how you are travelling, an individual Ziploc bag for each person filled with homemade trail mix can be a favorite tradition for all ages.

****

As children get older, daytime vacation activities may become more diverse among family members. Make the evening a time to reconvene and share the day's events.

****

If eating in while on vacation, take turns being the head chef who determines the menu and leads the preparation.

During a vacation, limit the use of electronics and television by all family members for at least a couple of hours every day and during certain group activities, such as meal time.

****

Create a travel food journal with illustrations. You may wish to rate the clam chowder in every restaurant in town, compare the pizza in each state you visit, note favorite ice cream stops or just judge local cuisine. Over the years, this will become a unique family memoir.

****

Take a family photo that helps identify the vacation location. Afterwards, give every member a small framed copy with the date and location written on the back.

****

Use online resources to create a calendar for the upcoming year, composed of photos from vacations and other important happenings of the previous year. These calendars become the simplest way to annually give each child their own concise scrapbook.

****

In new locations, have one evening at a restaurant become a taste-testing night. Everyone orders a different entrée with the understanding that all will be sampled. It can be fun and educational to role-play being food critics and guess the ingredients of each dish.

Purchase comedy CDs appropriate for all ages,
as group laughter sure breaks up a long drive.

****

As children become grown don't stop vacationing together
from time to time, but realize that parents are often still the
ones who have to get the ball rolling. The tradition of family
vacations does not need to come to a halt just because the
chicks have flown from the nest.

****

Determine a category of landmarks for your family travel
photos so that over the years you develop a running history
of trips with a themed background. Ideas to consider are
lighthouses, lakes, state flags, "Welcome" signs or an iconic
landmark or billboard for that location.

****

Start the tradition of a great car game. In the Alphabet
Game, each player finds and calls out the letters in order
from A to Z, as they see the letters on signs, trucks,
license plates, etc., outside the car window.
First one to call out "Z" is the winner.

****

Have your children start the tradition of a postcard
collection for places visited.

Have each child create a simple scrapbook, using a two-page spread per vacation to document their experience. Include ticket stubs, photos and a couple of their own sentences to journal. A weekend trip to Grandma's, a Boy Scout week at camp or going away with a friend's family all count, too. Following every vacation, find time to sit together and talk about the favorite sites, people, food and activities.

****

At the start of every long car trip, issue a pack of Life Savers to each family member (of appropriate age).

****

Be sure your family knows a handful of sing-along songs. This is a great way to break the monotony of a car ride. Patriotic songs and "rounds" are always fun choices.

****

Have each person choose their own Christmas tree ornament to commemorate a special trip or outing.

****

Bit by bit, have your child turn their bedroom door into a collage of summer vacation fun by attaching ticket stubs, brochures, maps, photos, etc., to the door. When the new school year begins, summer memories will be close at hand.

Your *Vacation* Traditions

_____

_____

_____

_____

_____

_____

_____

_____

_____

_____

_____

_____

_____

_____

_____

_____

_____

_____

_____

_____

_____

_____

_____

_____

_____

_____

_____

_____

CHRISTMAStime

I think it was when my sister and I were young teenagers that my mother's understandable Christmas Eve fatigue spawned a new tradition. Around that time, Laura and I were asked to help carry downstairs all the non-Santa wrapped gifts and put them under the tree in preparation for Christmas morning. No doubt there was an album of Christmas carols playing on the stereo that evening and pillar candles throwing a warm glow across the fireplace mantel to cinch the mood.

Once my husband and I had a child reach the age when he could successfully navigate walking and carrying a gift simultaneously, the tradition now known as "The Parade of Gifts" began in our own household. Each Christmas Eve, after dinner, church and last minute gift wrapping, my husband puts on a Christmas CD and sits by the tree to manage the influx of gifts from the parade. Before I start pulling out the wrapped surprises from their hiding places, or the kids grab their carefully created or purchased goodies for each family member, a parade route is determined. It is purposefully never the most direct path to the tree. Rather, it always requires looping around the house and stairs. No one is permitted to pass anyone else, there is no running, and regardless of the sizes, only one or two gifts may be carried each time. You would think all this structure would be a deal-breaker for the kids to have fun. You couldn't be more wrong. They read nametags and share excitement about the weight and shape of packages; they take turns, work as a team, and I succeed in stretching out the element of anticipation a little further. As a Christmas tradition, it has remained a favorite for the Mitchells for over 25 years and counting. That's a pretty good run!

In compiling this book, numerous friends apologetically said, "We really don't do much in the way of traditions, except..." And every time I heard the start of one of those sentences it always ended with a simple, beautiful family tradition that was far too undervalued. Remember, it is not about the quantity of traditions or the complexity of a single tradition that makes it successful. It is really about the simple joy it brings and the ease with which it can be repeated. Try to find a few ideas in those shared here to mold into your version of a tradition. Or perhaps this list will inspire you to just keep a sharp eye out for the budding traditions right under your nose. Even if you do not celebrate Christmas there are holiday ideas here that can easily be tweaked to fit your family.

Christmastime Traditions

During the week prior to Christmas, have family members help make batches of simple recipes like microwaved peanut brittle, sugar cookies or breads. Divide these into smaller quantities, tie up with lots of ribbon and deliver them on Christmas Eve to neighbors and friends.

Each year, choose a new ornament for each child. Create a small memory book that contains a photograph of each ornament and a short description of why it was chosen. When the child grows up and has their own home, you will be able to gift them this specialized set of ornaments and the keepsake book.

****

Always place a small Santa gift for each family member among the branches of the Christmas tree.

****

Before opening gifts on Christmas morning, everyone sings "Happy Birthday" to Jesus.

****

Each year, prepare the favorite breakfast casserole or coffee cake the day ahead for an easy and delicious holiday tradition.

****

Have all children wear matching PJs for Christmas Eve and Christmas morning. If possible, include Mom and Dad. Matching flannel pants with red T-shirts work, too.

****

Hand everyone a Santa hat to wear when it comes time for the tradition of trimming the tree.

Each December, roll easel paper out onto the floor and use precut holiday shaped sponges and paint to stamp out patterns for your own wrapping paper.

****

Evenly personalize some of the family gift tags i.e. "to our favorite 6th grader" or "to our inventive 12-year-old."

****

Leave out cookies, milk and carrots for Santa and his reindeer. The next morning there is sure to be only crumbs and the last stump of a carrot remaining.

****

To illustrate a "Giving Tree," have family members write on small tags any act of charity they did during the month of December. Some examples could be putting coins in a Salvation Army bucket, staying after school to mentor another student, purchasing an item for a toy drive, sending holiday cards to our enlisted men and women serving oversees or lending a hand to a neighbor in need.
Read the tags aloud; then add them to your tree.

****

On Christmas Eve, read aloud the enchanting book
The Animals' Christmas Eve by Gale Wiersum.

Attend a community tree lighting event every year, preferably one which includes singing carols.

****

If sending a holiday letter, have each member of the family sign their name at the bottom of the page before making your copies to mail.

****

Pack small plastic bags with dry dog treats, tie off with ribbon and deliver them to a local animal shelter.

****

Count down to Christmas with a daily Advent calendar.

****

In the toe of each person's Christmas stocking, place an orange, as a reminder to appreciate simple blessings.

****

When opening gifts, start with the youngest family member going to the tree and picking a gift to hand-out to someone in the family. Have everyone watch that gift be opened, before it is the turn of the next youngest person to hand out a gift, and so on.

Each year, place a gift or two on a low roof, in an outside tree or even just in the middle of your driveway. The magic of Christmas can be reinforced when a gift that fell out of Santa's sleigh is discovered.

****

Once ready for bed, gather around the Christmas tree in a dimly lit room (candles optional) for the reading aloud of *'Twas the Night Before Christmas.*

****

Every year make hot chocolate in lidded insulated mugs to accompany a ride around town to see the holiday lights. Be sure to bring along holiday CDs for a family sing-along.

****

Following Christmas morning, it's time to call long-distance relatives and share holiday cheer.

****

Never let your guests leave your holiday get-together empty handed. Keep it simple by giving out small containers of homemade sugared nuts or chocolate-dipped candy canes.

****

Each year, pick one holiday-related live performance for the family to attend. This is a terrific way to expose children to the fine arts and add another dimension to family fun.

Annually purchase an ornament for each child, add a short typed message about their past year by "laminating" it to the ornament using clear tape. Remember to note the year.

****

When the holiday meal is finished, remain at the table while each person takes a turn leading the group in their favorite holiday song.

****

Be in your own home for every Christmas morning.

****

Create some version of a gingerbread house every year.

****

Have grandparents, aunts, uncles, cousins, etc., come over on Christmas day in their pajamas for a casual lunch of homemade soup and bread.

****

Whether it is an egg frittata or a Swedish smorgasbord, find a special recipe, preferably related to family roots, to be part of every Christmas.

****

Every Friday evening of December, have a family screening of a holiday movie or television special.

Have a wrapping party for non-Santa gifts.
Divide the family into two groups to sit on the floor,
on either side of your bed. Put wrapping paper and bows
on top of the bed for all to use. Everyone is on their honor
not to peek over the bed while wrapping is taking place!

****

Every year add a new, framed, holiday photograph
to the family's larger collection that gets put out
on display each December.

****

Have your official Christmas dinner on December 26,
especially if Christmas morning fun at your house
runs well into the afternoon.

****

On Christmas Eve, each person opens a single gift.

****

During the holiday season, partner with a local family service
organization to fulfill the wish list of a family in need.
Get the entire family involved in the shopping,
wrapping and delivery.

****

Gifts from Santa are unwrapped but always labeled to the
child with "Love, Santa" on the gift tag – written
in one's non-dominant hand, of course.

Make garlands by stringing unbuttered popcorn and cranberries on thread. Use these to decorate an outdoor tree for the birds to enjoy.

****

Purchase a small, artificial tree to have the young ones decorate with all of their handmade ornaments.

****

Gather friends and go caroling each December.

****

Once all the holiday decorations are stored away for another year, sit the family in a circle and pass around the holiday greeting cards that have been received, for one last bit of enjoyment and appreciation. (Many assisted living facilities collect the fronts of greeting cards for various art projects.)

****

Have a family overnight camp-out around the Christmas tree.

****

Use the "Twelve Days of Christmas" to represent the "Twelve Days of Giving." Beginning on December 25th and ending on January 5th, have the family jointly do a different good deed daily for someone in need.

Your *Christmastime* Traditions

Additional HOLIDAYS

My grandparents lived in a beautiful stone house in Princeton, which was originally a pre-revolutionary tavern and remains a historic landmark today. Thanksgiving at their home was like stepping into a Norman Rockwell painting, and I adored it. For decades, Mabel and Edwin hosted the larger extended family each turkey day. Everyone came smartly dressed and with a home-cooked contribution for the holiday buffet. There was a large dining room table, attired with linen napkins, good silver and crystal wine glasses. And, for the seven cousins, there were two card tables placed at one end of the grown-ups table. Elegant table aside, my grandmother's true skill was the art of inclusion. For example, she would intercede if one aunt or uncle dominated the conversation too long by soap-boxing on politics or religion, and she would draw out the quieter ones at the table including her grandchildren, with earnest questions. I especially remember the look of dread that spread across the faces of those of us squeezed at the card tables when Grandma initiated the idea of each grandchild taking a turn after the meal (and while everyone was still seated) to stand and briefly share what constituted a normal day for them. I must admit this tradition had a short run of only a few years, as by the time it was begun, the cousins were all in the pre-teen and teen years of eye rolling, sighs and not wanting to be in the spotlight.

While in their early eighties it became too tiring for my grandparents to continue to host this multigenerational annual extravaganza. Simultaneously, the cousins were drifting toward their own Thanksgiving celebrations with spouses and new extended families. So we were all forced to redefine the holiday. There were growing pains, but there were new opportunities as well.

When Bill and I took over as host and hostess for our immediate family, we decided to carry on my grandmother's commitment to having everyone actively participate in the holiday. Our first step in that direction was to have our three young children join us in the kitchen to help with simple food preparations for the big meal. This bolstered a great team spirit and the bonus was that the children started learning some cooking skills, too. We also began the now favorite tradition of passing our son Greg's handmade ceramic heart around the table, for each person to hold while sharing aloud what they are most thankful for.

I have recently heard of a growing tradition called "Friendsgiving." The Sunday after turkey day, friends gather at one home, with left-overs and casseroles in-hand to celebrate the blessing of friendship. What a great idea! The following are ways that might help you to underscore your important family ties and friendships throughout the year.

Other Holiday Traditions

Prior to the holiday meal, have everyone in attendance trace their hand with markers to make a colorful, paper table runner.

****

Find and press the best fall leaves to scatter on the dinner table as colorful decorations.

****

Establish a gratitude journal in which every Thanksgiving attendee adds a few lines about what they are most grateful for that year.

****

Another way to include everyone at Thanksgiving is to have a single-sentence trivia fact hiding at each person's seat, to later share aloud with all during the meal. An alternative is to use Thanksgiving jokes and riddles.

****

Have each person write something they are thankful for on a large paper feather. Attach these to the body of a paper turkey (attached to a door or refrigerator) and later have fun guessing who wrote which one.

Creating name cards for the table is a fun and inexpensive way to get children involved in getting the table ready for guests. It also gives them a sense of pride for their obvious contribution.

****

Catch a family movie at noon. The season's blockbusters often come out on Thanksgiving weekend, and at that time there are few crowds and no shortage of fun.

****

Every year after the meal it is time for charades. All ages included, and "boys against girls" is often a good division of teams. Or, count off as in gym class with the odd numbers being one team and the evens becoming the other team. Another option is a rousing game of Pictionary using a large easel with paper.

****

To occupy restless children waiting for the Thanksgiving meal, hide a small toy turkey in the house. Each child needs to find it, without revealing its location to others. Once everyone has spotted it, dinner is served. "Hot and cold" clues can aid the youngest participants.

****

For Valentine's Day, bake a 9" x 13" pan of brownies. Once it has cooled-off, use cookie cutters to cut out heart-shaped brownies.

Make a Valentine mailbox by covering a shoebox with red
paper and heart stickers and cutting a mail slot on top.
Next to the box, put out small slips of paper with pens.
Family members are encouraged to write one signed
compliment per slip of paper for each member of the family.
This can be done repeatedly throughout the month of
February. On Valentine's Day, give them out at dinner to be
shared and appreciated. Later, store them in envelopes.

****

Make toast, cutting off the edges to create a heart shape.
Top with a little butter and some red sugar crystals
for a sweet Valentine morning.

****

For a full week surrounding Valentine's Day, have a family
"Random Acts of Kindness" campaign. With large, lined
easel paper taped to an inside door, have family members
write down the random kindnesses they do during the week.

****

On Valentine's Day, with the help of a bit of food dye,
the milk is pink. On St. Patrick's Day, milk turns green.

****

On the eve of St. Patrick's Day, children leave out a small
bowl of oatmeal at the back door for the leprechaun.
During the night, the oatmeal is eaten and in the morning

only an empty bowl and some gold glitter remain – bringing good luck for the year ahead.

****

Leprechauns will visit on St. Patrick's Day; you can tell by the way they mess up the beds and knock books to the floor while leaving behind a few powdery footprints and a small treat in a golden wrapper in each bedroom.

****

Try your hand at rounds of Peeps Jousting. This involves sticking a toothpick into each of two marshmallow Peeps, which belong to two different family members.
Place them on a paper napkin facing each other and microwave them until they grow big and one Peep eventually pierces the other.

****

Consider doing an egg hunt with some of the eggs labeled for individuals by name. Inside the eggs include a coupon for favorites like a trip to the movies, a pass on doing the dinner dishes, a "you-pick" dinner choice or an extended bedtime.

****

Have an annual raw egg throwing contest using two-person teams. Start with each pair close together and after each individual has had a turn throwing, then catching their egg,

each pair takes one giant step further back. The team
that gets the farthest distance between them
without breaking their egg, wins!

****

Write a message on a simple puzzle you buy or make, with
clues to where a child's Easter basket is hidden. The child
must assemble the puzzle to read the clue. A picture puzzle
of only a few pieces can work well for younger ones.

****

Breakfast Egg Wars: everyone chooses a hard boiled,
colored Easter egg for their breakfast. Going around the
table, have two people hit their eggs together. Continue
until all but one person's egg remains undamaged...really!

****

Each Earth Day, on April 22, plant a tree or work to
improve a garden or other green space.

****

On Earth Day, discuss re-purposing and recycling,
and come up with a one-year family "Green Pact" on ways
the family can conserve and reuse.

****

Gather the family to attend a Memorial Day parade.
Remember to bring along small American flags to wave.

Observe the National Moment of Remembrance each Memorial Day at 3 p.m. to remember and honor the sacrifice of those who have fallen in service to our country.

****

Create a flag cake by first frosting a sheet cake with vanilla icing. Add rows of halved fresh strawberries to create the stripes and fresh blueberries to make the field of stars.

****

Making homemade ice cream is bound to be a favorite tradition on the Fourth of July.

****

A family picnic followed by watching a fireworks display make for a very memorable July Fourth celebration.

****

Never miss having your trick-or-treaters collect coins for UNICEF (United Nations Children's Fund) while going door-to-door on Halloween.

****

New Year's Eve is synonymous with pulling out the box full of hats, headbands, horns and blowers. Everyone picks a hat for the evening. (String confetti is optional – but fun.)

A dinner of finger food and appetizers, paired with a big action movie for all ages and ending with a sparkling cider toast at the stroke of midnight is the recipe for a great family tradition to launch the New Year.

****

Follow the old German tradition of pork and sauerkraut for New Year's Eve dinner. Before the meal, guests wish each other as much money and good fortune as there are shreds of cabbage in the pot of sauerkraut. The pork is believed to represent abundance and signify good luck in the coming year.

****

On New Year's Day, lay out on the floor a five-foot long roll of easel paper. Gather the family, and with brightly colored markers, take turns writing down (at all angles) the family events of the past year under the title "Goodbye to (past year)." Be sure to include who lost teeth, got braces, played on a soccer team, had a recital, stayed overnight at Grandma's house, went on a trip, got a driver's license, received awards, special visitors, etc. Don't forget to include items about Mom and Dad, too. And, have everyone trace and label their handprint. After taping the finished product to an inside door to enjoy throughout January, roll it up and store. Eventually, you will have a whole box full of treasured family scrolls.

Your *Additional Holiday* Traditions

_____
_____
_____
_____
_____
_____
_____
_____
_____
_____
_____
_____
_____
_____
_____
_____
_____
_____
_____
_____
_____
_____
_____
_____
_____
_____
_____
_____

Closing Reflection

Having simple traditions sprinkled throughout your family's life will strengthen your family's identity and shared history. Although at times one might wonder what the difference is between a habit and a tradition, to me it comes down to one word: heart. A tradition is a repeated activity that impacts an individual's sense of self and how they are connected to others: family, friends and across generations.

Some of the smallest traditions can be carried in our hearts for a lifetime. I remember how my father's mom (a.k.a. Mum-mum) always had a little bowl of cashews waiting just for me, whenever I came for a visit. My mother's parents (a.k.a. Grandma and Grandpa) had their own tradition of ending each evening with a game or two of *General* – a version of Yahtzee they picked-up during their trips to South America. For the last five years or so of their lives together, they rarely missed their special game time at the end of each evening. It felt like such a privilege when I was able to share in these traditions with my grandparents. Subsequently, cashews and Yahtzee will forever represent so much more to me than the obvious; they will represent special people in my life.

A few years ago after a particularly hectic Christmas Eve day, I asked our three young adult children if they wanted to skip our annual Parade of Gifts. I suggested that since they were all getting so grown-up, perhaps this year we should just collectively bring out the gifts for under the Christmas tree.

Immediately all three chimed in that of course we would not break the tradition and that age didn't factor into it at all. As I write this our youngest child, Greg, is about to turn twenty-one, and we have yet to skip the "Parade" or the reading aloud of '*Twas the Night Before Christmas*. Our kids consider themselves lucky to have grown-up in a household with about a dozen or so annual traditions. They love that these traditions take them back to childhood memories and the warm feeling of family, despite the fact that they are all very busy spreading their wings in the larger world. These traditions are part of our family's legacy.

The point of my trip down Memory Lane is to illustrate how easy and simple traditions can have such a tremendous impact. It is never too late to begin; so what's stopping you? Get busy creating some traditions to share with the favorite people in your life. Everyone will be glad you did and the impact will resonate for years to come.

As mentioned at the start of this book, our daughter thinks my recent run on creating one-dish meals that always start with sautéing a chopped onion, is in fact a new family tradition. With that in mind, I have included four, now "traditional" recipes that prove her point. The last one however, comes from my mom. It seemed fitting that the person who most created traditions in my childhood should close out my book on that very topic. Thanks for the memories, Mom!

Sure Bet Beef

Serves 4

- box of Near East Couscous mix with Roasted Garlic: prepare as directed on package, set aside
- 1 large onion, chopped
- ½ sweet red bell pepper, chopped
- 2 TB olive oil
- 1 TB butter
- 1 lb. ground beef (or ground turkey), cooked, set aside
- ½ C. cooked corn
- 1 large tomato, chopped
- 1 TB dried parsley
- 1 tsp. dried basil
- 1 tsp. dried oregano
- ½ tsp. garlic salt
- 1 tsp. ground black pepper
- ¼ C. shredded Parmesan cheese
* Garnish: low fat sour cream or guacamole

In large fry pan, heat olive oil and butter over medium-high heat. Add onion and sauté for 2 minutes, before adding chopped pepper and cooking mixture until tender.
Stir in cooked ground beef and all remaining ingredients, including couscous. Mix well and heat through.
(Option: Add ½ C. spaghetti sauce.)

Top with a generous dollop of suggested garnish on each serving.

Helpful Hint:
If mixture gets too dry while cooking, add fat-free chicken broth a few tablespoons at a time, as needed.
* Serve with mixed green side salad.

71

Simple Oriental Shrimp
Serves 6

- 2, 10 ounce bags of Bird's Eye frozen white rice,
     with peas and carrots
     Prepare as directed, set aside
- 2 C. fresh steamed broccoli, then chopped
     (or one box of frozen chopped broccoli, cooked)
- 2 lbs. fully cooked shrimp, all cut in half
- 1 large chopped onion
- 2 + 4 TB olive oil
- 1 TB butter
- a small can of sliced water chestnuts,
     drained and cut in halves
- 2 to 4 TB of low sodium soy sauce
- 2 tsp. minced wet garlic (from jar or tub)
- ½ C. shredded carrots
- 2 TB oregano
- 1 TB lemon juice
- ground pepper to taste

In large fry pan, heat 2 TB of the olive oil and the TB of butter over medium-high heat, add chopped onion. Stirring constantly, sauté onion for about 4 minutes or until tender.

Add all other ingredients, using only as much of the remaining 4 TB of olive oil as needed to properly coat the mixture. Heat thoroughly, but do not dry-out shrimp by overheating.

* Serve with chilled fruit salad.

Turkey Meatball Medley
Serves 4-6

- 1 medium onion, chopped
- ½ sweet orange pepper, finely chopped
- 4 + 2 TB olive oil
- 1 TB butter
- 1 pkg. of fettuccini
- pre-cooked turkey meatballs, halved
- 1 large jar of spaghetti sauce (about 2 C.)
- 2 TB oregano
- 1 TB tarragon
- 2 TB parsley
- box or bag of fresh raw spinach
- garlic salt
- pepper
- garnish: grated Parmesan cheese

In 2 quart saucepan over medium-low heat, warm spaghetti sauce with meatball halves. Stir in the oregano and parsley.

In fry pan over medium heat, combine 4 TB of olive oil with the butter. Add chopped onion, sprinkle with pepper and sauté until tender. Remove from pan, set aside in a bowl.

Cook fettuccini per package, keep warm.

Using the previous fry pan on medium-high heat, warm the 2 TB of olive oil. Add entire package of fresh spinach and lightly mix and turn to achieve slightly wilted leaves. Promptly remove from heat. (Continued on following page.)

On individual plates, layer portions accordingly:
1. Fettuccine
2. Wilted spinach leaves, sprinkled lightly with garlic salt.
3. Add portion of onion and pepper mixture.
4. Add ladle of sauce and meatballs.
5. Pepper to taste.
6. Garnish with grated Parmesan cheese.

* Serve with a side of steamed French green beans.

<u>Helpful Hint</u>:
Do not overcook spinach or it will shrink down to near nothing. Use tongs to help lightly turn spinach while warming it enough to barely wilt.

Nancy's Seashells
Serves 4+

- 8 oz. pkg. of seashell-shaped pasta:
     cook as directed on package to al dente, set aside
- 1 large onion, coarsely chopped
- 4 TB butter
- 2 C. grated sharp cheddar cheese
- ½ C. (or so) of bottled chili sauce
- 3+ TB Worcestershire sauce
- Salt & pepper to taste

Melt butter in 5 quart fry pan over medium heat, add onion and sauté until tender.

Add all remaining ingredients and continue to stir until cheese is melted.

Serve promptly, to avoid sauce drying up.

Helpful Hint:
If mixture gets too dry, simply add a bit more cheese and chili sauce.

* Serve with steamed broccoli, sprinkled lightly with
   fresh lemon juice.

61634069R00049

Made in the USA
Lexington, KY
15 March 2017